STEM Projects in **MINECRAFT®**

The Unofficial Guide to MINECRAFT® Technology

JILL KEPPELER

PowerKiDS press

Published in 2025 by The Rosen Publishing Group, Inc.
2544 Clinton Street, Buffalo, NY 14224

First Edition

Editor: Greg Roza
Book Design: Rachel Rising
Illustrator: Matias Lapegüe

Photo Credits: Cover, pp. 1–24 Soloma/Shutterstock.com; p. 4 Africa Studio/Shutterstock.com; p. 6, 8, 10, 14, 16, 18, 20 Levent Konuk/Shutterstock.com; p. 5 Ique Perez/Shutterstock.com; p. 17 ju_see/Shutterstock.com; p. 20 V.S.Anandhakrishna/Shutterstock.com.

Cataloging-in-Publication Data

Names: Keppeler, Jill.
Title: The unofficial guide to Minecraft technology / Jill Keppeler.
Description: Buffalo, NY : PowerKids Press, 2025. | Series: STEM projects in Minecraft® | Includes glossary and index.
Identifiers: ISBN 9781499447019 (pbk.) | ISBN 9781499447026 (library bound) | ISBN 9781499447033 (ebook)
Subjects: LCSH: Minecraft (Game)–Handbooks, manuals, etc.–Juvenile literature.
Classification: LCC GV1469.35.M535 K46 2025 | DDC 794.8'5–dc23

Manufactured in the United States of America

Contents

Solving Problems

You might think of technology only as things like computers and smartphones. However, technology is anything that uses science to solve problems and the tools used to solve those problems. In other words, it's the use of scientific knowledge for practical purposes.

If you look at it this way, *Minecraft* has lots of technology! There are many problems to solve in order to survive, build, and explore. There are simple kinds of technology and more **complex** forms that may **involve** redstone, which is like a *Minecraft* system of electricity. You can learn about engineering, or how people create things using science and math.

Perhaps the simplest and earliest form of real-world technology was the stone hand axe, like the one shown here.

Tools Are Technology

A key part of surviving and building in *Minecraft* is making tools. These are mostly simple tools just like early humans made. In fact, probably the first thing you'll want to do when starting a new *Minecraft* survival game is to get enough wood to make a wooden pickaxe. This will take three wooden **planks** (from any kind of tree) and two sticks.

Then, use your wooden pickaxe to gather enough cobblestone to make some stone tools. *Minecraft* tools may be stronger depending on the material they're made of. Tool materials include wood, stone, iron, gold, diamond, and netherite.

MINECRAFT MANIA

In the real world, you really shouldn't punch a tree trunk. You'd hurt your hand! But in *Minecraft*, that's the first (but slowest) way you have to gather wood.

This would be a good place to **spawn** in *Minecraft*! There's lots of wood to gather to make tools.

If technology, including tools, is a way to solve problems with science, what problems can you think of in a normal *Minecraft* game? Pickaxes and axes help you gather stone and wood. What else do you need to survive? Food is one thing! A fishing rod (made with sticks and string) helps you get fish for food. A hoe lets you prepare dirt to plant crops.

Minecraft nights can be dangerous as monsters come out. If you can make a bed, you can sleep through the night. To make a bed, you need wool. To get wool, you can make shears with two iron **ingots**.

MINECRAFT MANIA

Use shears on a sheep to get one to three blocks of wool. You could also just kill a sheep to get wool, but that will only get you one block.

Minecraft sheep can naturally be white, black, brown, light gray, dark gray, or (very rarely) pink.

Strong, Stronger, Strongest

While wood is the first *Minecraft* material you'll probably use for tools, it's also the weakest. Wood tools will break faster than other tools and work more slowly. There are some materials they can't affect at all. For example, while you can gather stone with a wooden pickaxe in *Minecraft*, you can't gather any kind of ore other than coal and some copper.

The next strongest material for tools is stone. Gold tools can gather many things quickly but also break more quickly. Iron can gather most materials, and diamond can affect all those plus obsidian and a few other things.

MINECRAFT MANIA

Netherite is the strongest material you can use for *Minecraft* tools. You need to have a diamond version of the tools, a netherite ingot (made of netherite scraps and gold), and a netherite upgrade.

Gold armor is useful when you're in the Nether! Piglins, a Nether mob, will attack you unless you're wearing a piece of gold armor.

Weapons Are Tools

Some of the earliest human tools were weapons such as arrowheads and blades. You'll need these in *Minecraft* too. Even if you're not competing against other players, you'll need to hunt for food and **defend** yourself against monsters. You can use any tool as a weapon, but some work far better than others.

Melee weapons are hand-to-hand weapons. They include swords and axes. Ranged weapons attack at a distance. They include bows and crossbows used with arrows. You can use some **potions** as weapons too. You can throw splash potions that have various effects against monsters, animals, and other players.

MINECRAFT MANIA

You can craft most *Minecraft* weapons but not tridents. You can only get a trident if a drowned zombie drops one. They're both melee and ranged weapons.

To make a sword, you need a stick and two wood planks, gold ingots, iron ingots, or diamonds. This shows a player with a diamond sword.

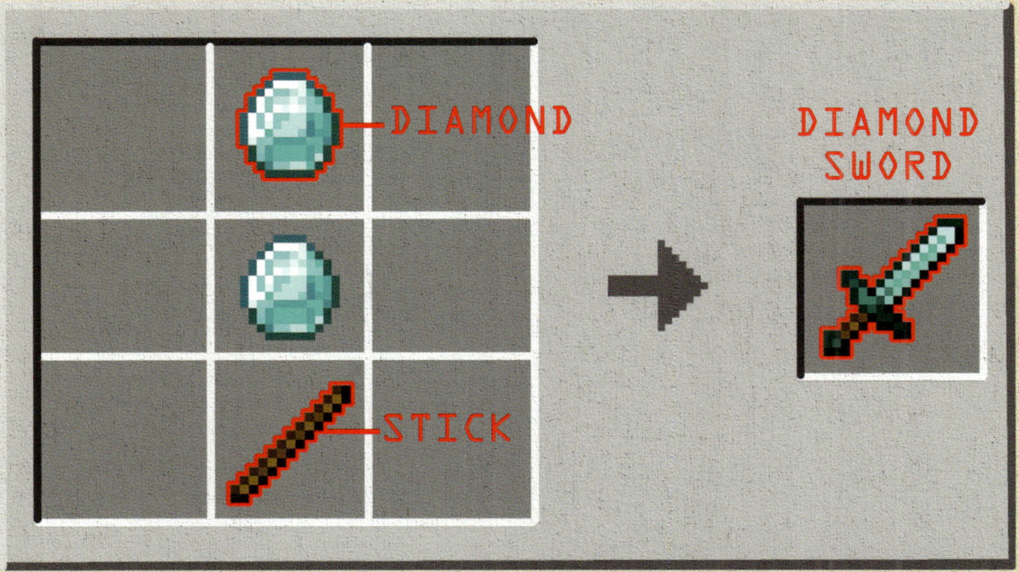

Fire!

Fire can be a tool, and it helped many early humans in the making of other tools. You can put fire to use through tools in *Minecraft* too. Campfires can cook food, provide light, and keep bees from attacking you. You can light them with a tool called flint and steel. You can also light uncontrolled fires with this tool, but that can be dangerous!

Smelting is changing materials through fire and heat. Furnaces, blast furnaces, and smokers all use fuel to smelt things. Furnaces can cook food and **refine** ores. Smokers just cook, and blast furnaces just refine ore, but both are faster than a regular furnace.

MINECRAFT MANIA

Torches are probably the first and most important way a player will use fire in *Minecraft*. They're made from a stick and a piece of coal or charcoal.

You can make a *Minecraft* campfire with logs, sticks, and coal. Campfires will send up smoke. If you put a hay bale under the fire, the smoke will rise higher.

More than Survival

As you play more *Minecraft*, you might want tools for more than just surviving. You might want to look for treasure or explore your world. In a similar way, the use of technology expanded in human history as people had time to do more than simply stay alive.

The invention of the compass opened the world to **navigation**. Real compasses point north. In *Minecraft*, a compass (made of redstone dust and iron ingots) always points back to your spawn point. However, you can change it to point to a lodestone made of **chiseled** stone bricks and a netherite ingot.

MINECRAFT MANIA

Clocks were another important real-world invention. You can make a *Minecraft* clock with four gold ingots and redstone dust. It will show you when nighttime is coming up so you can get to safety!

Compasses helped change a lot. If you always know where north is, you can figure out where other things are too.

Transportation Is Technology

The wheel is likely one of the most important pieces of technology ever invented. *Minecraft* only has one form of wheeled **transportation**: the minecart. You can make a basic one with five iron ingots. *Minecarts* must run on rails, and there are several different kinds of both minecarts and rails.

Boats are another important form of technology you can find in both the real world and *Minecraft*. People invented boats as many as 10,000 years ago! *Minecraft* boats are powered by the player through oars, just like some of the earliest real boats. You can make one with five wooden planks.

MINECRAFT MANIA

A walking *Minecraft* player moves about 4.3 blocks per second. A boat on flat water moves about eight blocks per second, as does a minecart on a powered track.

Each *Minecraft* boat can support two riders, but only a player can row.

Basics and Beyond

Most of *Minecraft's* technology is very simple. Still, once you get past survival and simple exploration, you can start increasing the tools and technology you control. You can use redstone, the *Minecraft* system of electricity, to make machines ranging from the basic to the **extreme**! People have even made computers in the game.

One basic redstone tool is a lever. It's very easy to make, needing only a block of cobblestone and a stick. Flipping a lever can provide redstone power (or turn it off) for blocks including doors and pistons. Experiment and see what you can do!

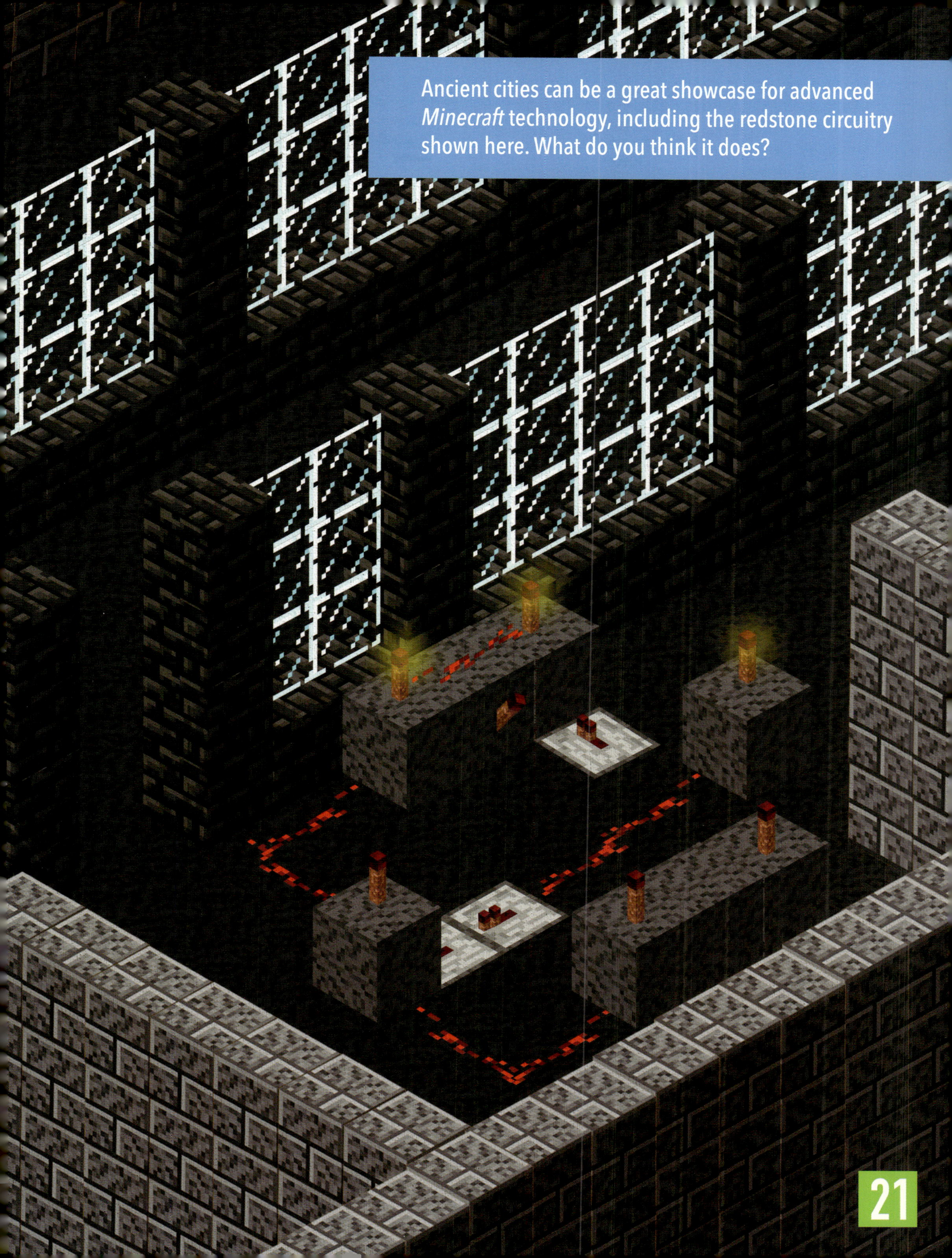

Ancient cities can be a great showcase for advanced *Minecraft* technology, including the redstone circuitry shown here. What do you think it does?

Glossary

chiseled: Formed as if carved by a chisel, or a metal tool with a sharp edge.

complex: Not easy to understand or explain, having many parts.

defend: To drive danger away.

extreme: Very great in degree.

ingot: A solid piece of metal formed into a brick.

involve: To make part of.

navigation: The act or process of finding the way to get to a place when you are traveling.

plank: A heavy, thick board of wood.

potion: A drink meant to have a magical effect on someone.

refine: To improve or remove extras from.

spawn: To first appear.

transportation: A way of traveling from one place to another.

For More Information

BOOKS

Miller, John, and Chris Fornell Scott. *Unofficial Minecraft STEM Lab for Kids.* Beverly, MA: Quarry Books, 2018.

Mojang AB and the Official Minecraft Team. *Minecraft Guide to Survival.* New York, NY: Random House Worlds, 2022.

O'Neill, Bill. *Amazing Inventions that Changed the World.* LAK Publishing, 2022.

WEBSITES

How Does a Compass Work?
wonderopolis.org/wonder/how-does-a-compass-work
Wonderopolis examines how a compass shows the direction.

Stone Tools
kids.kiddle.co/Stone_tool
Learn more about the stone tools that early humans used.

Tools
www.ign.com/wikis/minecraft/Tools
The IGN site provides more information on *Minecraft* tools.

Index